ABCs Of Grief

———— ❧❦❧❦ ————

Reclaiming Life After Loss

Loretta McCarthy

ISBN: 9781520537818

PUBLISHED BY DANCING TREEPEOPLE PUBLICATIONS
UPPER LAKE CALIFORNIA, USA
www.dancingtreepeople.com

A Gift for You:

Special Audio Meditation

Moving through Mourning

available at

www.lorettamccarthy.net/abcsgift

Dedication

Mom and Dad

John and Pat

With

Love and Gratitude

Foreword

For many years Loretta has volunteered in co-facilitating grief and loss groups as well as bereavement camps for families through Hospice Services of Lake County. She has taken her knowledge, education, training and life experiences and incorporated them into her book. She represents all aspects of grief, loss and transformation from A-Z in a creative and powerful way.

I call Loretta "The Closer." She has an amazing ability to synthesize what was expressed in the group, reframe the emotional content and pull it all together in a positive way. She has accomplished the same in her book in a compelling realistic manner.

She refers to her grief journey: "No matter how much time has gone by since the passing of my loved ones, there are still moments when I feel the sadness of loss rise up in me. Not with the same intensity but still profound and often tear producing. I know my task is not to get over the loss, though I treasure the feeling of having come through the deepest pain, because then I can feel the love more fully again. Then the future holds hope." Loretta weaves her life experience of transforming and understanding grief and loss.

Loretta walks alongside you in this book. She knows the path because she has walked it as well. Each path will unfold a little differently, a path that we often wish we did not have to walk. It is comforting to know we now have a book that is easy to relate to, validates our feelings, thoughts and lifts us up with hope.

Linda L Laing, LMFT,
Director of Bereavement Services
Hospice Services of Lake County

Table of Contents

Introduction

My first remembered loss was the death of my kitten when I was about seven years old. I hadn't even named her yet. She was a tiny ball of fur - very hard to see when curled up under the kitchen table in our cramped two-room apartment. It was an accident – my father's size 13 foot landing on her neck and taking her away from me. How it happened was not important to me. That it happened sent me into a tailspin of grief. A part of me shut down, as often happens when loss is a shock and the feelings of grief are left untended.

Years later I was able to mourn this loss – and the many others that have dotted my life. The most significant recent ones being the loss of my two brothers in 2012: John to suicide and Pat to Parkinson's and a heart broken by John's death. What I have chosen to write about in this book are snippets of wisdom that have emerged within me as I have experienced grief and mourned through each of my losses (and continue to do).

My willingness to open up and share with an experienced counselor: the frustration, anger, sadness, and yes, despair I felt during that first year after my brothers' death has made this book possible. I have also been enlightened and strengthened by the grief groups that I have co-facilitated in the last three years. I have been deeply touched and transformed by the evidence of resilience in the midst of ongoing struggle and the power of compassionate listening within a support group to bring healing and hope in the midst of profound sadness.

Finally you will notice that the chapters are not arranged alphabetically, even though the title speaks of ABCs. In my experience there is nothing orderly about the grieving process. Consider this is an invitation to go where you feel led as you begin to read this book, or start with the letter that matches the first letter of your name, or embark on this journey with chapter one. It is my desire that wherever you begin you will find solace and strength within the insights I have shared.

"If the condition of grief is nearly universal, its transactions are exquisitely personal." -- Meghan O'Rourke

1. Comfort

My dog Millie just jumped onto my lap. No use trying to explain to her that I am writing a book and trying to decide where to start! She wants to be petted and will not be denied. As I rub her gently and remind her that she is a good dog, my "where to begin" becomes clear. Start with comfort.

When we are in grief we seek solace and reassurance first and foremost. The difficulty is that we often resist the overtures of sympathy that others have to offer. Words, even kind, gracious actions, make no sense in the midst of the pain we feel. Yes, we are grateful for the initial calls and cards – and miss them when others have returned to life as usual. (Something that is not an option for us in our deepest grief.) But the comfort we seek is not primarily found in others, it is found in ourselves.

The gentleness we offer ourselves when the tears begin to flow as we wait in line to pay for our groceries. The choice we make to sit with the memories, which waken us in the night, and sip a hot cup of herbal tea while again tears wend their way down our cheeks. Allowing ourselves to schedule a massage or Reiki session, even though we know that tears will be part of that experience as well.

Sleep may be hard to come by during our time of grief, so an afternoon nap might give us some real rest and relaxation. Preparing for bed in the evening, even when we do not feel tired, and allowing ourselves to lie down with quiet music in the background may open up a time of deep sleep. Or we may simply read or write in our journal and let our bodies respond to sleep as it comes. We realize that relaxation is as important as sleep. Sometimes sleep, like butterflies and happiness, appears when we stop chasing after it.

The comfort we need comes in the guise of extreme self-care. At the beginning when the grief is still raw and unfathomably painful, there may be only one kindness we are able to offer ourselves each day. So we start there. Extra rest, walking near a flowing creek, sitting by the window and watching the movement of birds or trees, enjoying our favorite dessert and, yes, petting our animal companion.

"I come into the peace of wild things who do not tax their lives with forethought of grief... For a time I rest in the grace of the world, and am free." -- Wendell Berry

2. Dosing

*In the past few years I have had the privilege of co-facilitating a number of Hospice bereavement groups. I have learned a lot in these eight-week encounters with people who are walking their grief journey faithfully in spite of the pain. Having been caught in a prolonged downpour without an umbrella, I understand the feeling of being deluged and bedraggled. At times in my own grief journey I felt so overwhelmed and emotionally drenched that the thought of ending my life to stop the anguish crossed my mind a few times. The suggestion to take the grief **in** doses helped me to cope.*

We are not meant to deal with our grief in one sitting or even in a specific period of time. Even though the common wisdom encourages us to make no major decisions for at least a year, we know that mourning our loss cannot be given a fixed timetable. It is different for each of us who grieves. But one thing is true for all of us, dosing supports our process.

Even with full-blown allergy symptoms, we still follow the bottle's recommended dosage. Taking two or three or even four tablets at a time when the label says one every 24 hours will not help us to feel better. It may even worsen our condition or cause additional problems. The same is true concerning how we treat our grief. We handle what surfaces in doses. Dosing will keep us from feeling more overwhelmed than is manageable.

When anger, hopelessness, or fear come unbidden and threaten to overtake us, we need to stop whatever we are doing and pay attention. Denying or resisting our emotions will not stop them. Neither will our attempting to take them in and experience them all at one time. We need to go slowly and breathe deeply and trust that we will make it through this grief, even though we will never be over the loss as if it never happened.

When possible we allow our feelings to surface a little at a time. Though initially this may be difficult, progressively we will find the intensity of grief lessening. We can choose the path to take and even the activity and amount of time we want to devote to being with our grief. We make time to look at photos, sort through clothing, or go to places filled with memories of our loved one. Usually having a supportive companion with us creates an atmosphere that empowers us to feel what we feel without being overcome by the feelings. But even alone, we can decide when have seen or done enough and tenderly stop for a while.

"Find a place inside where there's joy, and the joy will burn out the pain." --Joseph Campbell

3. Kindling

During the winter months we heat our entire home with a soapstone wood burning stove located in the living room. Because the house is relatively small and very energy efficient, this is easy to do – once the fire is started! For me, kindling is the most important part of making the fire happen. So in the late summer and throughout the fall months, I spend time picking up small dry pieces of wood and stacking them in a bin close to the house - easy to reach when the fire starting time arrives. It is amazing to watch the twigs and sticks catch fire, building a momentum that then engulfs the larger pieces of wood and eventually sparks the logs into a full-blown conflagration. Voila! Warmth spreads throughout the house.

Our thoughts while we are grieving tend to focus on the absence of our loved one – the many ways in which life is empty and meaningless for us now. We may ruminate on the circumstances of his/her death, or dredge up ways in which we could have been more compassionate, or replay in our mind conversations that caused friction. We know that this kind of thinking is ineffectual, even depressing. We may want to shut our mind down. Thinking is just too painful – too agonizing. But how do we do this? Gather "kindling"!

Slowly we begin to search for words that bring us a sense of hope, even while we are caught in the throes of hopelessness. "Love alone will last." "All will be well." "Support from unknown sources will see me through." When our thoughts move towards the negative we take a deep breath and gently replace them with wisdom words. Since our minds focus on one thought at a time, "I wish I had . . ." can become "I am grateful that . . ." We light the small positive kindle thoughts and allow them gradually to spark a new sense of wellbeing.

We can do the same with our choice of reading and listening materials. Finding a book that comforts us, leaving it near where we sleep or relax, provides us with a source of inspiration when our thoughts become dark and bleak. Or listening to calming, reflective music rather than the chatter of conflicting thoughts may bring us to a place of peace. It is not a matter of forcing ourselves to think happy thoughts. That would never work. Rather we open ourselves up to the flames of promise, trusting that in due time hope will catch fire again within us.

None of the above is easy. Often our grief makes reading and listening to anything unpalatable, especially when they are suggested by other people as a means to help us get "over our loss", which is not possible. However, when we remain open to finding the right kindling for us, wisdom will come to us and assist us in the process of grieving our loss.

11

Loretta McCarthy

"There is a sacredness in tears. They are not the mark of weakness, but of power. . . . They are the messengers of overwhelming grief, of deep contrition, and of unspeakable love." -- Washington Irving

4. Openness

Deep within me there is still a piece of pain when I remember the words that told me of my older brother's death: "Loretta, John is dead. He killed himself." I no longer feel the instant urge to scream, "NO"! Years of mourning have helped me accept his passing as a reality. But I still remember and miss him everyday. And that is good. I realize now what a gift it was to open myself up to scheduled meetings with a local Hospice grief counselor as I walked through this period of profound loss.

Loss of a spouse after 55 years of marriage, of a daughter whose life held such promise, of a son who struggled with addictive behaviors most his life, of an animal companion faithfully by our side for 15 years, the list is endless – each loss is accompanied by a choice: Will we open up and trust again? Will we let ourselves love again?

And yes, openness is a choice. Everything in us wants to heal our loss and at the same time wants to be left alone with our grief, hoping that the pain may keep us connected to our loved one. We can stay closed down or we can open up and share our struggle with someone who is qualified to walk with us on our journey.

We may even benefit from participating in a grief group, where we share our stories and listen to those of others in an atmosphere of non-judgmental acceptance and loving trust. This is not always easy to do at the beginning of our grief. But when we begin to feel isolated and maybe stuck in unhealthy patterns, we may recognize the need to reach out to others who are experiencing similar circumstances.

We make this choice with an awareness of what is best for us in this moment. Always the touchstone is: Will this group eventually bring us to a place of peace and deepen our understanding in ways that will move us forward through our grief? It may be more difficult in the beginning, but gathering with others who are grieving can be a source of renewed hope.

"Some pain is simply the normal grief of human existence. That is pain that I try to make room for. I honor my grief." -- Marianne Williamson

5. Mourning

Until I read Alan D. Wolfelt's book, <u>Understanding Your Suicide Grief</u>, I used the words "grief" and "mourning" interchangeably. Still do at times! However the distinction has helped me in the process of dealing with my losses and seems worth sharing. Grief is our internal experience of the loss: the thoughts and feelings that we carry within us as we miss our loved one's presence. Mourning is the outward expression of our grief: the tears we shed, the words we share with others about our loss, the ways in which we memorialize our loved one.

For me, the difference was significant because it allowed me to make choices about how to mourn, even while I honored the grief I felt within. I did not have to feel "better" inside before I began sharing the loss I was experiencing.

At the beginning of the bereavement process, grief has a grip on us. Understandably as the word "bereave" means "to deprive of, take away, seize, rob." We have been robbed of a relationship that was a significant part of our life and we feel bereft. Inside it feels as violent as the word "seize" sounds. The pain often intensifies before it begins to lessen.

Only mourning loosens the clutch that grief has on our heart. Until we are able to express the sadness, loneliness and lost-ness we feel, grief will control everything we do and think. This expression does not have to be public, though most of us benefit from the compassionate presence of others as we mourn. Nor does it need to follow a particular pattern. Each grief is unique and so the mourning process needs to be personalized.

We may cry copious tears or we may write an angry letter to our loved one and then burn it. Both are valid expressions of the grief we are feeling. We may choose to visit the burial site often or not at all. What we do is not as important as why we do it. Our personalities, as well as the character of our relationship with our lost loved one will guide us as we journey through our singular grief by mourning the loss.

The only likeness our mourning will have compared to others is its importance as we seek to recover from loss that has deprived us of the person who has died. We can learn from others ways of mourning that may be helpful. Not all of us would think of setting up a punching bag as way of letting go of anger or of writing a song to honor the life of our loved one. If we are drawn to someone else's mourning strategy, we may try it ourselves. Most likely our approach will end in a very unique result.

"It takes strength to make your way through grief, to grab hold of life and let it pull you forward." -- Patti Davis

6. Balance

My mother struggled to maintain emotional balance throughout her life. In her 70's she claimed the refrain, "Don't worry be happy" as her motto. This helped her somewhat with the chronic depression that plagued her days and nights. In her 80's after her radiation treatment for breast cancer Mom decided to seek psychological counseling. Her choice was truly a gift to herself in her elder years. She found someone who listened to her and taught her to hear and accept her deepest truth.

Because of the onset of Meniere's disease (a chronic illness that affects the inner ear and has no cure), Mom also suffered from a physical imbalance from her mid-60s until her death at 86 years old. She walked very carefully feeling afraid of a fall that might cripple her and take away her independence. Her frequent experiences of vertigo frightened her and led to her being very cautious especially when walking on uneven surfaces. Mom stopped trying to keep up with Dad as his long legs hurried ahead of her. She adjusted to her limitations and chose a slow and steady pace that felt secure and safe. She listened to her needs and adjusted her life to meet them.

When deep grief enters into our lives we often feel as if we have lost our footing. We are afraid even to walk down familiar paths for fear of getting lost or falling into a dark hole. Our mind may try to reason with us and tell us otherwise but our emotional and physical self is still fearful and untethered.

What was once easy and done as a matter of routine is no longer simple or even desirable. We lose our ability to focus and to undertake tasks that formerly required very little attention. For example, we no longer feel like preparing a meal and even resist eating a delicious one offered by a friend. We find ourselves out of balance and do not know how to regain the sense of wellbeing that was part of our life before the loss.

It is here that we benefit most by listening to our wiser self. Maybe we remember what we told our friends or children in the past about staying focused on what is healthy in times of difficulty. For a while we may just go through the motions of eating healthy meals and occasionally calling a friend to share our feelings and sadness. Eventually we do adjust to our new way of being in our world without our loved one's presence. It takes the time it takes and only happens if we keep trying to move forward until the new path becomes clear.

"Opportunities to find deeper powers within ourselves come when life seems most challenging." -- Joseph Campbell

7. God

Foghorn is a welcome addition to our orchard. Ever since our rooster Hank III died a few months ago (most likely carried off by a coyote) our hens had been confused and restless. So a few days ago when our neighbor's rooster arrived looking for a place to stay, it was a real blessing. We called our neighbors and told them that Foghorn was standing by the fenced-in food forest where the hens are housed asking to be let in. They gave us permission to keep him and life in the chicken yard has been peaceful ever since. Even the egg output has increased!

Everything in our life changes when a loved one dies – everything, including our relationship with **God**. Whether we speak of God, Goddess, Higher Power, YHWH, Divine Spirit, etc. or claim there is no God, all of us experience a shift at the root of our being. This is painful and baffling. When we need a sense of security, most of what sustained us in the past seems gone.

Our time of grieving is filled with questions. Many of them are addressed to God and most remain unanswered! We may have a few pertinent queries for doctors or nursing home personnel and even challenge a family member on their behavior toward our lost loved one. But the big questions, we save for God and they usually begin with "Why . . .?" They are often filled with undertones of anger and are riddled with frustration and hopelessness. This is normal and an integral part of the grieving process.

As time goes on, most of us become resigned to the fact that our questions are not going to receive a response. Something shifts within us and we stop asking. Maybe we read of another person's experience and understand how they found their spiritual footing and decide to reconnect in a new way. A book recommended by a friend or a moving quote on Facebook opens up a path that leads to deeper peace. Or our loved one comes to us in a dream and we feel consoled. Slowly we begin to believe in Love again and little by little our questions need no answers.

Loretta McCarthy

"I wasn't prepared for the fact that grief is so unpredictable. It wasn't just sadness, and it wasn't linear. Somehow I'd thought that the first days would be the worst and then it would get steadily better - like getting over the flu. That's not how it was." -- Meghan O'Rourke

8. Patience

A little over three years after my brother John's death, I was washing dishes by the kitchen sink when a bird flew by the window with a huge worm in its mouth. Going back to the nest most likely to feed her young! Later in the day I noticed a dandelion ready to release its seeds into the air at the next wisp of wind. That evening as I wrote down my daily list of gratitudes, I became aware of how many small sightings had entered my life on this one day. How different this day's experience was from the early days of my grieving when nothing seemed to matter and even the sunniest day appeared gray and lifeless.

When we are grieving, people try to tell us that we will feel better one day, maybe even soon. We don't believe them. It is hard to imagine that the emptiness, the loneliness, the rage, or the anxiety will ever end. We "know" it will always be this way and we have no idea how we will go on living. It is absolutely impossible for us to conceive a change.

In the midst of the permanence we feel, we benefit greatly from inviting patience to be our companion, even if in the present moment we do not understand how this will help. We do not have to change our minds or convince ourselves that what we are experiencing will end. We may continue to feel lost and miserable each day as we grieve. However patience practiced daily - with ourselves, our fluctuating feelings, and other people around us – provides us with opportunities to shift our belief in what the future without our loved one will be like.

One morning or a late evening hour we may become aware that our breathing is less shallow when a memory of our loved one surfaces. This realization is another gift that comes from our willingness to follow the patience path, rather than giving into frustration when the loss feels overwhelming and endless.

We can choose to listen to the voice of patience reminding us of small changes already taking place and trust that more will follow – maybe? We may write the same feelings down in our journals over and over again and then notice a slight movement toward a release of pain, and offer ourselves thanks for being patient with the grieving process.

"The friend who can be silent with us. . . who can stay with us in an hour of grief and bereavement, who can tolerate not knowing... not healing, not curing... that is a friend who cares." -- Henri Nouwen

9. X-ray

In 2009 I had cataract surgery – right eye then left - both had complications – not the responsibility of the surgeon – just the poor condition of my eyes. Stressed and anxious after the first surgery, I refused to change my daily schedule. Adjustments felt like weakness. I wanted to be strong and healthy. I wanted to see as well as other patients claimed they did. My thinking was not reasonable: "If I act better I will be better." But still I followed my mind's advice. Which is why I fell and broke my wrist!

One evening as I was bringing the mail into the house I found myself facing directly into the setting sun. I couldn't see anything, but I kept walking. Of course, I tripped and fell. The mail went flying into the air as I headed straight for the ground. An x-ray showed the damage to my wrist, luckily not too severe. The doctor's description of the delicate nature of the bones in the wrist as we looked at the x-ray convinced me to change my schedule to allow for needed healing – of my eyes and also now my wrist.

When we are grieving we often find it difficult to be attentive to our body's need for nourishing food, adequate rest, and daily exercise. We know the importance of each and yet we may resist making them a priority during the grieving process. Maybe if we could see an x-ray of our entire body, we would experience its beauty and complexity from the outside in. We would treat our body as the artistic masterpiece that it is. We would see how everything is connected and how each part of the body depends on the presence and health of the other parts.

Unnecessary x-rays are not recommended, but as we move through the grieving process paying attention to our bodies is a choice we can make each day. We may find it helpful to plan our meals for the day as we dress in the morning. Gathering the main ingredients and having them ready for preparation can serve as a reminder that today we choose to eat well. Arranging to eat with a friend so that we are not always eating alone, or trying a new restaurant so that we are not flooded with memories at a past favorite haunt, may ease us back into a habit of nourishing our bodies.

Our inner being desires rhythmic patterns. Our bodies crave motion to express these patterns. We are part of a movement larger than our own life – including our relationships with Earth and the universe. Especially in times of loss we yearn for a steadfastness that embraces the chaos we feel and turns it into safety and assurance. We may be drawn to the ocean. As we walk and listen to the water, we experience the ebb and flow of the tides and realize our life is much like that. Or we may decide to cycle on a path through the woods and find peace in the circular motion of our legs that gradually propels us into a world new and fresh. Sitting and staring out the window while we grieve may be part of the solution, but so is using our muscles and ligaments and bones to help us integrate the loss into our lives. Whatever form it takes, daily exercise is a source of healing for our grief.

"Love recognizes no barriers. It jumps hurdles, leaps fences, penetrates walls to arrive at its destination full of hope." -- Maya Angelou

10. Letting Go

It is very quiet in the house today, except for an occasional thump of Jose's hoe against the ground as he removes weeds from the food forest next to our home. Weeds have a purpose and, at times, can be quite beautiful and beneficial. For example, plantain, which is considered a weed by many people, is actually an herb. It is edible and also an amazing natural medication for bee stings and other bites. Plantain is abundant on our orchard, as is poison oak. Being highly allergic to poison oak, I have to be extremely careful to avoid contact. Just in case, I have a small arsenal of remedies readily available.

When we are grieving our emotions run rampant. We feel loneliness, sadness, despair, fear, and anger. Some times all these and even more feelings emerge at the same time. There may seem to be no reason for what we feel, until we are able to make a connection. We are sitting in an auditorium watching our daughter graduate from college and the tears flow – deep sadness has overtaken us. And then we remember, our life partner is supposed to be sitting next to us but his/her death has made this impossible. We feel what we feel. The way out is to feel the feeling as fully as we can.

Emotions call us to be present to the reality deep inside us. Like weeds, we may try to remove the ones that are too painful to feel, but they have a purpose. As we move through the mourning process, loneliness motivates us to seek new connections. Anger shows us how to speak our truth and end co-dependent behaviors in ourselves. Fear invites us to take up practices that provide us with a sense of safety and security. Like our willingness to receive a deep tissue massage, letting go of resistance to feelings brings healing.

Some feelings call for a different kind of letting go. Though we talk about feeling regret, or shame, or guilt, we need to handle these emotions differently from the way we walk with our sadness or anger during our time of grief. Regret, shame, and guilt are rooted in judgment and need to be uprooted as soon as possible. We don't need to mull over them or think them through and definitely not feel our way through them. We need to notice them – much like watching birds soaring in the sky – and then let them go.

"Grief doesn't have a plot. It isn't smooth. There is no beginning and middle and end." -- Ann Hood

11. Judgment

I have learned many things since I moved to an organic walnut orchard eight years ago. One lesson in particular stands out – maybe because I have learned it over and over again. When living in the midst of growing things one's work is never done and never the same. Grass mowed grows again; eggs collected means new eggs need gathering the next day; one year the harvest is abundant and the next year sparse; husk fly and ground squirrels seem to multiply at will; and the list goes on!

I have learned to be kind to myself as the farm manager – not to judge whether I am a success or a failure based on the outcome of my endeavors. Rather I make the best choice in the moment, see the task through to completion and trust the results will work out for the best.

So it is when we are grieving, there is no place for judgment. We cannot compare our process with anyone else's, nor can we permit a sense of failure to "get over ourselves" take root. Each day we open our hearts and our minds to feel what we feel, to be in the present moment with or without tears, and allow our mourning to take whatever shape seems best for now.

We may go for a long walk in the woods or by the ocean and let memories of our loved one wash over us. We may decide to visit a friend or family member who also misses the person we grieve and share stories and tears, along with a cup of coffee. We may choose to help out at a soup kitchen or volunteer at the nearby library and give ourselves a break from the daily remembering and mourning.

No judgment! All is well! Each step taken prepares us for the next step. The way in which we mourn is unique to us because the relationship we mourn was also unique.

We may decide to stay very busy for a while or do nothing at all. Our need for space and time may seem like isolation to others, but we choose to do what brings us peace. We know the difference between the loneliness that comes from mourning the passing of someone we truly love and miss deeply and the deliberate separation from the life that flows around us.

The most important path we can take is to treat ourselves as a loving parent would treat a child. No criticism: "You should do this." "You shouldn't do that." No judgments: "When will you get a grip on your emotions?" "Aren't you over this loss yet?" Yes, people really do say these words. Our response is to follow the main commandment of life: "Thou shalt not 'should' on thy self."

"I think you have to deal with grief in the sense that you have to recognize that you have it, and say that it's OK to have all the sadness." -- Ann Richards

12. Unplug

I just came in from the orchard where I was doing what I do most days in the spring - removing "suckers" from the walnut trees. Though the task is tedious and repetitive, it is very important for the trees. In its eagerness to grow the tree seeks to create extra branches usually at the bottom of the trunk. However, the suckers take needed energy from the tree's main purpose: nourishing the seeds within the husk so they can become walnuts.

When we are grieving, one-on-one or group encounters may drain our energy. This happens at a time when our vitality is already at low ebb. For example, we walk away from conversations feeling depleted, not energized. We need to pay attention to what is happening around us that we find exhausting. And then we need to unplug.

Unlike removing suckers, we do not need to remove all people or circumstances from our life while we are mourning, but we may need to unplug certain ones. We need to release ourselves for a while from connections that drain us, so that our energy can be used for our main purpose: healing the deep wound that our loss has caused.

Friends, even family members, relate to us differently in our time of sorrow. Some are supportive and sensitive. Though their presence does not lessen the pain, their caring comforts us. Other people offer us sympathetic words that often remind us of a Hallmark card selected to send to someone "in a time of loss". We are grateful, and maybe a bit annoyed, especially if the person is a close friend, but we understand how difficult it is to hold another's pain.

Where the most important unplugging needs to happen is with people who try to fix us. Some times with platitudes: "She is in a better place." "God needed him in heaven." Or even a cruel comment: "Aren't you over this loss yet?" We do not need to expose ourselves to words or actions that pour salt into our wound of loss. So we unplug – maybe for a short while until we are stronger. Or in some instances, we may choose never to plug in again.

No matter how other people react to our grief, it is essential that we realize their response is more about them that it is about us. When a person is uncomfortable with our grief and wants it "over" soon, it is often due to their inability or unwillingness to process their own losses in a deep and meaningful way. Our task is not to change them, but to focus on our own journey – and to choose not to bring them along – at least for a while.

Loretta McCarthy

"There is no grief like the grief that does not speak."-- Henry Wadsworth Longfellow

13. Yelling

I screamed into the night, "Noooooooo!" as I sat up in my bed awakened from a dream. The yell came from an abyss within me that previously I had never touched. In my dream kittens were being discovered – dead – throughout the house. Yelling "no" was the only appropriate response. Amazingly no one heard my crying out, but I felt it reverberate within my body.

Fortunately I was in a situation where I had the time and guidance to work with the dream. Twenty-four years after the loss of my kitten I processed my grief – holding my little seven-year old self gently as she cried pent-up tears. I did not know then that my loss at age seven was deeper than the death of my new pet friend. Twenty-years later I allowed the memory of being sexually molested at age seven to surface. Again only a loud yell of "Noooooooo!" would suffice.

Most of us have been cautioned about being too expressive. When we are grieving we may feel constrained by the presence of others who are also grieving. Or we may feel compelled to be "strong" for others who seemingly need more support. Whatever holds us back cannot be permitted to stifle the screaming, yelling, moaning, and groaning that yearns to be expressed. Everything in moderation has its place, but when we are grieving the best remedy for pent-up emotions is release.

That is why "yelling" is so important! We have to move beyond our comfort zone concerning how we express emotions so that the feelings can come forth from us. For most of us our yelling stopped when we entered into adulthood. No more temper tantrums! Stomping our feet at disappointment ended as well. But when we are in the throes of loss we may encourage this seemingly outlandish behavior in order to accomplish our goal – moving through our grief in all ways possible.

There are safe places where yelling may go unnoticed, e. g. in our car, at an understanding friend's house (away from a crowded neighborhood), in the middle of the forest, or in a vineyard. It may not have to happen often –once or twice may be sufficient. Quite like smashing plates against the side of an abandoned building to release anger, yelling as we deal with the pain of loss may have a soothing effect that thrusts us forward.

"No one ever told me that grief felt so like fear." -- C. S. Lewis

14. Earthquake

Recently I experienced my first California earthquake. It only lasted 15 seconds – a very long drawn out fifteen seconds! The epicenter was about ten miles away from my home, so the 5.1 on the Richter scale felt decidedly stronger for a novice earthquake "survivor". As the rolling movement of the house – and everything in it – continued, I had two simultaneous thoughts: How long will this last? What am I supposed to do?

Being in control seems very important to us when the chaos caused by grief overtakes us. We make statements: I cannot take any more of these feelings. I wish this were over – now. We ask questions: Will I ever feel differently? How long does this ache of loss last? And the most frightening question: What if I never feel okay ever again?

Grief places us very close to the epicenter of an emotional earthquake. Sometimes we feel the rolling motion in our body. It can cause a nausea that hinders us from even wanting to eat. But most often we experience the unsettledness in our core sense of being. Nothing is steady. Nothing is as it used to be. Our emotions roll over us creating angry outbursts or fits of crying that overwhelm and scare us.

Here the "What to do in an earthquake?" advice is helpful. Drop! Cover! Hold on!

Drop! We fall on our knees, admitting that we are powerless to control the flow of our grief. At the same time we connect with that which grounds us: memories, friends, beliefs, etc. We journal. We talk with someone who understands. We imagine. We choose hope over despair.

Cover! We need to feel sheltered and protected as we grieve. Surprisingly one of the best covers we can secure for ourselves is to express our feelings honestly and clearly. Beginning the process of mourning our loss creates a sanctuary where we can place even the strongest and most difficult feelings that arise. We may fashion a small altar in our home where we place mementos connecting us to our loved one. Here also we can place words or symbols that describe what we are feeling. As counterintuitive as it may seem, when we allow our vulnerability to show in a safe environment we are strengthened.

Hold on! Sometimes we can only wait through the sleepless night for the dawn to come. When we have done this often enough, we begin to realize that the dawn will come. So it is with our grieving. A week passes, then a month, followed by a full year and we remember our loved one's day of death. We begin to feel differently – not necessarily better, just different. What surrounds us now calls for our attention and we are able to respond more fully. All we can do is hold on until the dawn of hope and new joy appears on the horizon. And it will!

"Grief is characterized much more by waves of feeling that lessen and reoccur, it's less like stages and more like different states of feeling." -- Meghan O'Rourke

15. Alignment

My first and final driving lesson with my father lasted about five minutes. It ended abruptly when I panicked, frozen in the driver's seat, as the car veered and headed straight for a fire hydrant. Dad miraculously stopped the motion. We quietly changed seats and never mentioned my driving again. Ten years later, when I was twenty- seven, a friend with lots of patience taught me how to drive. Since then I have learned a lot about cars: how to change a tire, clean battery terminals, use jumper cables, and most important when to take the car to a mechanic for needed repairs and adjustments. For example, though I know when a car is out of alignment that is one job I would never do on my own. It requires skills and equipment that I do not have.

Dishes stacked up in the sink, bed unmade, phone messages deleted without a response - a few signs that we may be feeling depressed as we journey through the grief process. Or maybe opposite symptoms – nothing out of place, trying to keep everything in our outer world exactly as it was before our loved one died, or refusing to let the tears flow. Whatever the outward manifestations are, our feeling lost and depressed is a normal part of grieving – to a point!

We may hear ourselves say: "I wish I could die and be with him (her)." Or "Life is not worth living any more. It is just too hard." We may stop eating or engaging in activities that formerly brought us joy. Or we try to lighten our spirits with a hot cup of tea, a brisk walk, a conversation with some one who cares and understands and still the deep sadness continues. All this is a normal part of grieving – to a point!

It is not easy to write about this, nor do most of us feel at ease when we read about the importance of seeking professional help when our emotional life needs alignment. On our own we will continue to veer off course, wearing down our inner resources, and eventually we may skid off our path and make a choice for death, not for life. We may have many reasons for not calling on psychological or psychiatric assistance when we are dealing with prolonged, intense depression, or a compassionate friend suggests that we make at least one appointment. Most us know the reasons are often excuses because we are afraid or exhausted or . . . the list is endless. Only our yearning to be whole and healed can move us beyond excuses/reasons into the office of a caring professional for re-alignment. Hopefully we will foster that desire in ourselves and in one another.

"I work grief and sadness out of my body when I dance, and I bring in joy and rhythm." -- Inga Muscio

16. Intuition

When I was about eighty-five percent finished with writing this book, I stopped. Totally! I had been enjoying the process, finding the words flowing easily, and feeling that my insights were worth sharing. Nothing had happened. I just no longer felt like writing, so I put my work on hold, unsure of when or if I would begin again.

A small voice inside my head tried to convince me that I was wasting time. I was so close to finishing, why cease now? But I did. And then, after a month or so, I decided to look over the outline for the remaining chapters with the hope that I would be encouraged to start again. It worked. I got excited about finishing and I realized that one important piece had been missing - one simple word – "yet".

Paying attention to our heart voice - trusting our intuition – is very important as we grieve. It is also one of the hardest things to do. Our world has been turned upside down by our loss and we may feel that we cannot trust anything or anyone, especially ourselves. After all we may have decided that we are unable to protect or help our loved one, so we question our ability to make good decisions or find solutions to immediate problems.

Following our intuition does not mean we choose never to sort through our loved one's clothing and share them with a nearby thrift store. Or change the message on our answer phone indicating that this used to be a residence for two people. Or spread his/her ashes that have a place of honor in our home. It does mean we choose not to do this – yet!

Of course "yet" could turn into "never" and we may need help to sort out our resistance. But when our first refusal to take action surfaces, we need to respect ourselves enough to stop and sit with the feelings, not deny or override them. We might say to ourselves, "I am not ready to open the closet or go through the storage locker – yet." Honoring our intuition will open us to the next insight that comes and we will begin to trust our gut once again.

Eventually we will wake up one morning and be ready to do the sorting and the letting go of things in a nonviolent and thoughtful way. We will call our family and begin planning the memorial service that was delayed because we were not ready – yet. We will cry when the tears come and we will remember joyful times and fun places. Most importantly we will have re-established our relationship with our heart voice – knowing that we can trust ourselves and now live in this different world with peace and joy.

"It is by going down into the abyss that we recover the treasures of life. Where you stumble, there lies your treasure." -- Joseph Campbell

17. Release

My brother John was an extremely sensitive person – thoughtful and generous. He was also gruff and demanding – so much so that his behavior irritated lots of folks, including people who loved him dearly – like me. As I mourned his loss, I recalled the times when I was less than patient and I felt deep sadness with a twinge of guilt.

The fact that he took his own life angered me. I had assured him the day before that I would care for him in his elder years and that he was welcome at the orchard where I lived with my partner. Still he slit his wrists and ended his life. I was pissed! As the initial rage lessened I remembered how John had responded to my anger in the past – with tears. I began to realize that an important task for me in the mourning process was releasing myself from the guilt I felt and also releasing John from the burden of responsibility for the pain his action caused.

Whether we journey with a loved one through a long illness that culminates in death or we experience the shock of a sudden loss, there is often a need to release ourselves and our loved one from guilt and blame and shame after death occurs. We may be gifted with the opportunity to say final words of forgiveness and/or release, but most often there is not enough time or awareness in the moment to say all we would have wanted to convey. It is consoling to have spoken gently to our loved one as the end nears,

"You can leave now. I will be okay." But many of us who grieve did not have that chance – or found ourselves unable to do so at the time.

As we walk through our grief we can use our imaginations to accomplish what we could not do in real time. Instead of filling our mind and moments with thoughts of inadequacy "Why didn't I say . . .?" we can use helpful techniques to achieve a profound sense of freedom for ourselves and also release for our loved one. We may enter into a time of guided imagery quietly bringing our loved one's presence into our heart and saying all we want to speak now. Using our dominant hand we can craft a letter to the one whose loss we mourn, pause for a few moments at the end, and then write with our other hand a response from our loved one to us. Or we may choose to write down the thoughts that were unspoken and then burn them in a small ritual fire.

Whatever we choose to undertake as a means of releasing, we are affirming the necessity and importance of loosening the chains of regret, self-reproach and culpability. The difficulties and challenges of such exercises are worth the freedom we may feel afterward. Nothing takes the pain away, but some practices alleviate its intensity.

"Grief can be the garden of compassion. If you keep your heart open through everything, your pain can become your greatest ally in your life's search for love and wisdom." -- Rumi

55

18. Viewpoint

It was the beginning of fall in 1984 when I went to be with my parents as Dad's cancer became more aggressive. Some how the beauty of the New England autumn was lost on me that year. There was too much fear and anxiety – too many unknowns. I ignored the changing colors as I drove to the hospital daily - once again to find my Dad in pain with very little attention from the nursing staff. I still remember the words of one nurse. "We are an acute care facility. There is nothing more we can do for your father." Anger overwhelmed me. How could I notice beauty?

Dad was transferred to another facility in January of 1985 and during the spring I spent time each day at the window in Dad's room looking out at the nearby woods. At first my intention was to take a break from the intensity of watching Dad sleep and wondering if this breath would be his last. But as the days passed by I began to notice the appearances of tiny bits of green. Then I realized that the shades of green were amazing and varied. As summer approached I counted five, no ten, no fifteen tints of green. Noticing the gracious care my Dad was receiving and looking out the window at the cascading colors – all green and all so different – I felt peace in the midst of sadness.

We have all heard the statement: "It's all about mind over matter". Most of us respond with a skeptical look and a cynical, "Sure". We know we cannot change what is with our thoughts. Or even by thinking differently. Or can we?

Would a new viewpoint, as we grieve, help us to think in an unprecedented way? If so how do we find the new point of view?

By paying attention to what surrounds us and to what is unfolding within us. This may mean picking a bouquet of flowers and placing them in a place of honor within our home. And then watching as the beauty deepens, then fades and finally diminishes into death. And then planting the seeds!

Or we may watch as one season gives way to one another or notice the change in daylight and nighttime hours as the weeks pass by. Our viewpoint changes when we acknowledge dying is a part of living and loving means losing. We recognize that our grieving is part of a bigger reality and while it is painful, it is also shared.

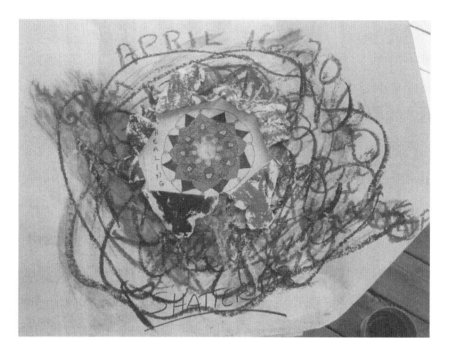

"Grief is in two parts. The first is loss. The second is the remaking of life." -- Anne Roiphe

19. Surrender

Journaling was an absolute necessity and a lifesaver for me after the death of my two brothers in 2012. Though what I wrote was often repetitive, it was so healing to put the words on paper rather than keeping them inside where they would often fester and become toxic. Recently I re-read one of my entries addressed to my brother John: "When you died my life got upended. More because you took your life than that you died. I keep wishing that I had noticed more or that I had flown home right away. I know that I am not responsible for your choice, but I feel so bad that your last days were so hard for you."

No matter how our loved one died – suddenly in an accident, or while playing basketball on the court, or after a long fight with cancer, or a gradual diminishment with dementia – one feeling surfaces in most of us who grieve: regret. Our inner and outer conversations begin with "if only or "I wish that." And our dialog with ourselves often ends with a list of "shoulds" especially at the beginning of our grief journey.

Partly it is a form of denial, but more importantly it is an expression of the need we feel for control. If we had only done such and such our loved one would not have died. Why we think we have so much power is not necessarily the best question to ask. Rather our task at this point in the mourning process is to surrender, which is easier said than done!

What helps us to let go of control? A practice like this may assist us. When we hear the "what if" words either inside us or spoken outside of us, we pause, take a deep breath, and replace them with "I did my best". At first this may seem like an artificial fix, but it takes us down a different inner road – one that eventually will lead to acceptance of our inability to make anyone's life different from what it is or has been.

It is important that we do this with gentleness and self-love. In time we hopefully will understand we only have control over our life, and even there our power is limited. But in the breathing and surrendering, we may find peace. Breathe in: acceptance and breathe out: need for control – daily and deeply.

"It is during our darkest moments that we must focus to see the light."
-- Aristotle Onassis

20. Tribute-making

In the spring of 2000 I participated in the Phoenix Project conducted by Dr. Jack Miller. Because it began only a few months after my mother's death, this 12-week intensive grief recovery program was especially helpful. It provided me with significant tools to use in my process of mourning. It also changed my life forever. It was here I learned the value of rhythmic structure and creative expression, not only as a path through grief, but also as a way to live more fully.

Initially I worked with finger paints and craypas. Then I moved on to barbed wire. Yes, forty-two feet of barbed wire! It was a very difficult medium to work with but perfect for my first tribute. The one I used to commemorate my forty-two years as a Sister of the Blessed Sacrament with all the losses I had experienced. With gloves on and wire clippers and glue gun in hand, I formed a tumbleweed-shaped structure. Beginning with 1958 and slowly moving forward I attached words and mementos at significant points – first to signify the losses and then to honor the blessings those years had held for me. My hands were slightly cut at times, but the tears I shed were those of grief – for painful good-byes left unspoken, for lost opportunities, and for love denied and unsought.

Tribute-making is a powerful tool for sorting through our grief. We remember the person (or another important part of our life now gone) in her/his total reality. We seek to capture their core. We strive to memorialize the essence of this person as best we can. Out of our memories we chose to create a tribute that honors "who" this unique person is for us. We touch points of pain: arguments left unsettled, choices to disengage, years lost through separation, or personality traits that annoyed. We also recall joys shared: trips to favorite places, dreams fulfilled, children raised, or projects completed.

The tribute may be something concrete: life insurance money used to dig a well so as to provide water for the future, a video that captures who this person truly is/was in our life, or a wall hanging that shows the trajectory of this individual's life journey with all its ups and downs. The choice is ours. For through its creation we seek to express our relationship with our loved one.

It is the time we take to focus on the person we are mourning that brings healing. Time and energetic attention spent remembering and releasing the grief we feel allows us mourn the loss that grips our heart. Whatever we choose to create as a tribute it will be accompanied by tears and at times intense emotions. By producing something in our outer world to represent our loss, we find a path through the inner pain we are experiencing in our grief.

"Tears are the silent language of grief." -- Voltaire

21. Wonder

In August of 2013 my partner and I packed up our car and headed on a three-week tribute journey honoring my brother John. We were bringing his ashes to a site on the other side of the country – a place that was dear to his heart. We journeyed six thousand plus miles (going and coming back). Our plan included stops at the many places John had visited on his annual summer trek across the United States to assist at Earth centers.

Some thing remarkable happened inside of me during this tribute journey. The stone blocking the door of my heart was rolled away. Maybe it was the shared tears as I met so many people whose lives had intertwined with John's. Maybe it was the sense of closure as we laid his earthly remains to rest. Maybe it was watching the changing scenery outside and recognizing that beauty is and cannot be caught except in a fleeting moment. As the trip concluded I noticed I was no longer asking "why?" Now the question was: What if my life still holds more, even though my brothers are gone?

We cannot make this happen but it does. One day in our grief journey we begin to think – not only about the past (our lost loved one) or the present (our life filled with missing and sadness). We start to wonder about our life in the future with a sense that it may still hold more. At first this may seem like a betrayal, but gradually we understand that our choice to live again also honors the love we feel for the one we grieve.

No one will ever replace the family member or friend who has died. But we may invite another to enter into the life we are reclaiming. So we call a friend to reconnect and we realize that we feel a new bond growing. We open ourselves up to companionship. We may even choose a deeper level of intimacy that we thought would be impossible ever again. Always our heart is opened more deeply when wonder is allowed to be and to flourish.

Wonder comes with an element of caution as well as marvel and splendor. Moving slowly and paying attention to how we feel is essential. After all the grieving heart can seek what is new precipitously in order to avoid the pain of the present. So we choose to dance – moving forward, standing in stillness, drawing back – all done with a conscious attempt to be present to ourselves and to the person with whom we feel an affinity.

"You must do the things you think you cannot do." -- Eleanor Roosevelt

22. Quest

This morning I tackled a big job – washing the cobwebs and dirt off the north side of our house. Taking the garden hose and climbing carefully up the ladder, I turned on the sprayer. I watched with delight as the water cascaded down the wall, not only cleaning the surface but also creating multiple rainbows within the flow. I did not expect such a treat, but I truly welcomed each splash of color that appeared.

I was reminded of the butterflies and rainbows that crossed my path after my brother John's death. At first I chose to ignore them – pretending that I did not notice them. For me, both were symbols of hope and of new life. In the initial stages of my grieving I had no room in my heart for hope or promise. So I denied their existence. Gradually I began to recognize the appearance of the rainbows in the sky and the butterflies in the bushes as signs of companionship. They were not meant to make me feel better. Their purpose was to be and by coming into my line of vision to be with me in my time of sorrow.

When we lose someone we love, no matter what kind of spiritual path we are on, everything changes - sometimes very quickly. Spiritual nuggets, which were significant before, sound hollow and meaningless. A place that offered nourishment for our inner being – our soul – now seems empty and even distasteful. When we are grieving even the presence and companionship of friends, family and others who are supportive does not satisfy the loss and longing we feel deep within.

We have a choice – one that we make gently and when the time feels right. Are we willing to go on a quest that may lead us to a deeper understanding of life and death and life reclaimed? This quest may begin with a simple choice to pay attention to the colors we see around us – maybe seeing how many shades of red or yellow or blue dot our landscape. Gradually we may attach a meaning to each color: red – passion, yellow – light, blue - peace, etc. Then we may choose to ask for that gift to be in our life as we mourn. An opening, a request, a prayer!

We may seek to learn more about mystical traditions that have sought answers to the life questions that plague us as we grieve. Or we may explore root beliefs that sustained our ancestors. Grief enfolds us with primal pain and tapping into our indigenous soul may assist us on this journey.

If quiet times are difficult for us, we may explore musical forms that have the power to center us and move us through our times of tears. Whatever we are feeling in our grief, the choice to connect with an untried, or to revisit a familiar, spiritual tradition may open new doors to understanding.

"Grief releases love and it also instills a profound sense of connection."
-- Jacqueline Novogratz

23. New Normal

With the birth of my brother Pat in 1944 we became a family of five – true to the definition - a nuclear family. For many reasons, including distance and dysfunction, our contact with our extended family was very limited, especially in our younger years. Most of what we did – vacations, birthday parties, and other activities – we did as a family of five.

In 1985 my father died and we became a family of four. Though we had grown up by then and were living our own lives, we still coalesced around our mother until her death in 1999. In her waning years there was one constant that Mom spoke of with love and passion: "I have three great kids. Be good to each other." This became a mantra for us. It brought each of us multiple blessings, especially as we continued now as a family of three. Pat was married and had a family of his own so his experience was a little different. For John and I our concept of family remained the three of us – Mom's "great kids".

It is hard to explain how bereft I felt when my brothers both died in 2012. I no longer felt as if I had a family, even though I was an integral part of my life partner's family. Something had radically changed and I was alone in a deep down sense – bereft of what had defined me in the past.

When a loved one dies – or when we lose someone who has been a significant presence in our lives either positively or negatively – we often struggle to redefine ourselves after their death. Who are we now? With this relationship ended what does it mean for our life going forward? How can we reconcile what is in the present with what we have known in the past?

Before we can answer these and other questions, we need to be with the pain of loss that permeates our being. We need to acknowledge the differences and sit with the consequences. Attempting a quick fix may thwart the discovery our new normal. Like the nine months of pregnancy, we await the birth of our new self while we undergo the changes that being pregnant brings – as patiently as possible.

There does come a day when we feel differently. Maybe our feeling of being connected stretches to include another realm sometimes called "heaven" and we experience the closeness of our loved one in a way that surprises us. Or we resign ourselves to our new reality and at the same time are overwhelmed by a sense of gratitude for all that has been ours in the past. Whatever happens eventually we recognize the new normal that is our life after loss. We find our footing again and move forward with a sense of purpose that in our earlier days of grief would have seemed impossible.

"Deep in their roots, all flowers keep the light." -- Theodore Roethke

24. Zone Zero

In the spring of 2011, I participated in a Permaculture Design Class. Five weekends filled with information and experiences that (among many other things) taught me about patterns found in nature as a way to live here on Earth more respectfully and sustainably.

It was here that I first learned about "zones". Zones are used in permaculture design planning for placing elements according to how often we need to visit them. Areas that are visited every day (e.g. the vegetable or herb garden) are located nearby the house. Whereas fruit trees are located further away. At the center of all the planning is Zone Zero – where the human dwells – where the heart fire burns!

Our daily life does not stop when a loved one dies. Maybe for a few weeks we can stay home from work or school, skip some regular meetings, or make excuses for not getting tasks done. But sooner or later we step back into the world. It is here that we need to be sure we are attentive to what is happening in Zone Zero – our core being.

Our relationship with the one we lost to death is unique. No one else can claim to have known or experienced that person in the same way. We may find it helpful to share our memories with someone who also knew our loved one.

Sometimes we may find a listening ear and loving heart that is able to hold our stories and our tears gently even though they never met the one we lost. For these people and moments we are grateful.

But most of our work with sorrow takes place deep with our broken human heart. It is here that the mending process needs to happen. It is here that our focus and attention turn daily, even while we are out and about walking in the world again, minus the physical presence of the one we grieve. How do we keep the hearth/heart fires burning in zone zero with out permitting the conflagration to destroy us?

We are patient with the process. We invite "grief" to sit with us in front of the hearth. We welcome sorrow, not as a stranger that we do not like, but as a friend who will open vistas within us that we have never known before. We seek ways to creatively express what we are feeling through journaling, drawing, and/or movement. Or we sit in the silence, breathing deeply into and through the pain. We remember. We wait. We stay at home with all the feelings and emotions that surface. We learn to trust that healing will come. We will never be over our grief, but we will come through it one day.

"As you say goodbye to lingering disappointments and unattended grief, you will discover that every person, situation and painful incident comes bearing gifts." -- Debbie Ford

25. Harvest

My Dad spent the last six months of his life in a cancer care unit at a Jewish rehabilitation center where he received amazing care. I was able to be with him on a daily basis. So I witnessed firsthand his transition from pain to peace, from body ravaged with colon cancer to pure spirit embracing each day as gift, from my father to gracious child of God. By just being there I shared in a harvest of blessings. Even though the abundance didn't shine through in the moment, I have come to know the gift that time with my family around Dad's bedside held for all of us.

Maybe not in the early days of our grieving, but as the days, weeks, and months pass by we realize more fully the lessons we learned and the gift that being with our loved one on their last journey brought to us. We no longer take our health for granted for we know that in an instant everything can change. We find a treasure trove of patience within us. Being slighted or ignored by someone we considered a friend does not affect us as it formerly did. Life takes on a new perspective. Most importantly we understand how short our life span really is even if we live for a hundred years or more.

In other words, we begin to recognize the abundant harvest our loss and grief bring to us. We experience the rhythm of life so clearly seen in nature. The seed in the soil dies and gives birth to the tree. As the tree grows into maturity, buds appear and become blossoms. Blossoms fall apart to allow the fruit to come forth. When the fruit ripens we harvest and enjoy the taste and texture of all that has gone before. It takes time but eventually the abundance surfaces. We begin to feel deep gratitude and a lessening of anguish. Our mourning through grief has moved us from bud to blossom and beyond.

"Our human compassion binds us the one to the other - not in pity or patronizingly, but as human beings who have learnt how to turn our common suffering into hope for the future." -- Nelson Mandela

26. Future

I have travelled a lot in my 75 years of living. A few times I had very little time to prepare for the trip. Occasionally there were delays and complications along the way. But one thing was always true. My trip began in one place and ended when I arrived at my destination. This has not been the case in my journeying through the land of loss and grief.

No matter how much time has gone by since the passing of my loved ones, there are still moments when I feel the sadness of loss rise up in me. Not with the same intensity but still profound and often tear producing. I know my task is not to get over the loss, though I treasure the feeling of having come through the deepest pain, because then I can feel the love more fully again. Then the future holds hope.

First, we need to believe there is a future after loss, and then:

We **find** our footing in a new land – different but full of promise.

We **understand** that our loss is based in the love we have felt and seek to love again.

We **trust** that life will unfold with abundance and blessings yet unseen.

We **untie** knots of regret and guilt, if and when they arise within us – and they may from time to time.

We **remember** those who have gone before us and those who are with us now with gratitude and appreciation.

We **envision** the day when we reach out to another in grief and share the wisdom we have gleaned from our time on this journey.

May we be blessed in all the **FUTURE** holds for us!

Suggested Helps for our Journey though Grief

Hope-filled Reminders

Quiet times and spaces can be challenging when we are grieving. Our thoughts when we are alone may need to be redirected in ways that are healthy and calming, rather than depressing and dark. Finding a picture (or two) that open us up to hope may, for a moment, focus our minds beyond the pain of loss we feel and help us feel safe.

Placing the picture on the bathroom mirror may be a reminder in the morning and throughout the day that one day we will have come through the deepest grief and will know joy again.

Or using the picture as a bookmark in a book we are currently reading may also help us remember.

Images of hope, as well as photos of our loved one and places visited together, strategically placed throughout our home can lead us to peace and tears of release as we mourn.

Guided Imagery

Our imaginations can be both a hindrance and a helper when we grieve. When we fear what has not yet happened and wonder how we will handle situations without our loved one, we are creating more distress and difficulty for ourselves in an already very stressful time.

Making time to sit in a comfortable place, maybe with music playing softly in the background, and allowing our imagination to take us on a creative journey of discovery can help us heal and connect with love and life again.

The following are two examples meditations / guide imageries for times of grief:

Moving through Mourning 1 (A Gift Received)

During times of deep grief and sorrow we often forget to breathe fully and freely. Our breathing can become shallow . . . constricted.

So as we begin this meditation, turn your attention to your breath. Breathing in . . . breathing out . . . gently . . . slowly . . . allow your breath to become deeper and more prolonged. Breathing in . . .(one, two, three, four). Breathing out . . .(one, two, three, four) Breathing in . . . Breathing out . . . Breathing in . . .Breathing out . . .

As you continue to breathe deeply, imagine you are sitting in a familiar, safe place . . . with your inner eyes look around . . . become more and more comfortable . . . more and more relaxed.

As you relax, imagine there is a box on your lap - the size of a shoebox . . . it is beautiful. Notice the colors . . . any designs . . . the shape. Imagine picking the box up and becoming aware of its weight and any unusual features.

Putting it back down on your lap, you hear in your heart an invitation to gently open the lid and see what is inside. You pause for a moment . . . and take a few deep breaths . . .

You know that inside this box is a gift for you from your loved one . . . the one whose loss you are grieving. When you are ready, open the box and look inside.

Whatever it is . . . it is gift . . . be with the feelings that arise . . . if tears come let them flow . . . be with this gift in whatever way feels comfortable for you . . . for as long as you wish . . . remembering to breath and be grateful for the gift you have been given.

Moving through Mourning 2 (Flowing Like a River)

Choose a time when you can spend fifteen to twenty minutes alone without interruption – away from your usual routine and your cellphone or computer.

Go to a place where you can sit (or lie down) and be comfortable – a quiet space – a place that holds memories of peace for you.

Loretta McCarthy

Settle in gently - setting an intention to spend this time with whatever feelings arise – remembering that healing unfolds with awareness and acceptance.

When you are ready to begin take a few deep and prolonged breaths. Breathing in and out – allowing your body to relax – letting go of tension as best you can.

Imagine that you are sitting by a river watching the water flow slowly by – just be there by the river – watching it ripple and flow by gently.

Now imagine that you enter into the water and become one with the river. Let go – relax – all is well. You and the river are one - as you flow gently. Enjoy the flow and the quiet rhythm of being the river.

As you flow – notice the rocks that jut out of the riverbed and block your passage – maybe even slowing you down as you flow – rocks or obstacles that cut into your flow. What are the blocks that surface as you mourn – memories of words unspoken – regrets of actions taken or words said – desires for things to be different – anger with the way you feel or disappointment with responses from others.

Name them and flow over and around them and then gently let them go.

Notice the banks of the river where some branches have fallen into the river – as you flow over the branches – remember the many ways in which the loss of your loved one has changed your life – other relationships that have ended – possibilities for your life that no longer exist – dreams that may have died with your loved one.

Name them – flow over and around them and then gently let them go.

Continue to flow peacefully – being the river – gentle and powerful – flowing under the trees or through the pastures – wherever you flow notice any signs of life that are along your banks – flowers, animals, people in the distance. As you see them remember the evidences of hope that have been present in your life as you move through your time of mourning.

Name them – flow by them and then gently let them go.

When you are ready – return to being you – sitting by the river – no longer in its flow. Become aware of your breathing - take a few deep and prolonged breaths. Breathing in and out – remembering what it was like being the river – flowing gently and powerfully.

In whatever way is comfortable for you bring your time to a close – gently acknowledging that healing unfolds with awareness and acceptance.

Simple Tributes

Memorial tree

Planting a tree in memory of our loved one can be a healing action.

Journaling about the experience may deepen our sense of connection with our loved one for years to come. Recently I came across my journal entry around the tree that I planted for my brother Pat three years ago. Tears flowed. The healing continues.

I planted a tree today in memory of my brother Pat – an Angel Red ™ Tree Pomegranate. I dug the hole and then invited Denise over to check on its depth and width, so that the roots would have the needed room to grow. Carol, a friend who was visiting, came over to the food forest as well to offer a prayer over this symbol of Pat's life.

How good it was to have this spontaneous gathering to honor the life of Pat, the "gentle giant". The words we said could not convey all the feelings, but the simplicity and the authenticity of our presence together held the deeper meaning. I was very aware of the guardedness I felt. It seems easier, at times, to just shut down and do something, like planting a tree. The moment of remembering was surrounded by numbness within me. I wanted it to be a profound experience. It was what it was: a tribute to Pat whose loss I grieve deeply.

The trip to Oak Valley Nursery in Ukiah to pick up the pomegranate tree satisfied a need in me as well. Denise was away so I went on my own. I had called ahead so the owner was expecting me. Gruff and kind rolled up into one would be a good description of him. I heard his voice, "Can I help you?" before I located him slouched down in his truck. His movements were slow, but purposeful as he unfolded his frame and stepped out of his vehicle. When I mentioned that I was looking for pomegranate tree he seem to recognize my request from the

Loretta McCarthy

phone call we had. "Do you want a bush or a tree? Same fruit — different shape!"

*I thought about Pat who had never traveled too far from Brockton and in an instant decided — a pomegranate **tree**. I wanted something that would grow tall and branch out, not stay close to the ground and be **bushy**. Removing one gangly sapling from the soil in a nearby bucket the salesman offered to prune it before packing it for the trip in the trunk of my car. I was grateful and willing to wait while he took care of a customer on the phone and then hunted for the pruners.*

I thought of Pat as I waited and watched. Though not a nursery owner, Pat was skilled at what he did in the leather dyeing business. I could imagine the people that might have come to the place where he worked with questions and needs that he would have responded to with ease after decades of experience. Pat, like this man, was an elderly person with unbelievable knowledge walking around familiar surroundings with no pretensions, just doing his job as always. I wish I had asked this salesman / owner his name.

Montage of Memories

When my friend Mary died my heart felt deep sadness and profound peace. What a life she lived! How much was now missing from Earth with her presence gone as I had experienced it! I wanted to somehow express my feelings of gratitude and loss.

Simple, readily available materials can create a meaningful memorial that is easily framed. A calendar picture for the background – cut up, placed creatively, and then pasted onto a firm piece of paper or light cardboard. Words cut out of magazines that capture the spirit and life of our loved one placed around a copy of a favorite photo. A light covering of "mod podge", once dried, gives the montage stability for framing.

Memory Space

Gathering photos, souvenirs, objects that were important to our loved one(s), or reminders of love shared and then placing them together in one spot gives us a place to focus our remembering. We may call it an altar of memories or a sacred space. Whatever the name, it is a way to honor the life we shared.

A Gift for You:

Special Audio Meditation

Moving through Mourning

available at

www.LorettaMcCarthy.net/abcsgift

About The Author

What does it take to form a woman of wisdom and compassion? Loretta McCarthy, aka *Earthwalker*, shows us one possibility. Gently combine these three ingredients: the

fidelity of fifty years as a Catholic Sister, the blessing of serving within a culture different from her own, and the courage at age sixty-eight to leave the convent and follow the call to love another person intimately and completely for the rest of her life.

Recognized as a spiritual leader within her religious community, Loretta received training in Spiritual Direction at the Institute for Spiritual Leadership (Chicago, IL). Her years of ministry as a spiritual companion and retreat guide culminated in the founding of an urban house of prayer in Atlanta in 1990. During the fifteen years Loretta spent at Maisha House of Prayer she offered to the people of the city and beyond: a prayer presence and a place for deep healing. It was there that she honed her skills as a listener, spiritual companion, and group facilitator. In 2014 she was initiated as a Ritual Elder of the Phoenix Project (an international 12-week grief recovery program offered by Dr. Jack Miller).

Loretta McCarthy

Loretta presently lives with her life partner in Upper Lake, CA on an eleven acre walnut orchard. She is a writer, spiritual companion, and grief counselor with Hospice Services of Lake County. To keep her life real Loretta manages the farm, provides companionship for two dogs, cares for the chickens, and volunteers with local organizations that assist people with food securities needs.

She also serves those on life's journey by offering **Sacred Listening Sessions** and **Healing Our Losses Experiences** to individuals and groups.

Also By Loretta McCarthy

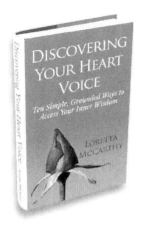

Discovering Your Heart Voice: Ten Simple, Grounded Ways to Access Your Inner Wisdom

Available on Amazon.com

In her first book: ***Discovering Your Heart Voice: Ten Simple, Grounded Ways to Access Your Inner Wisdom***, Loretta draws on her life experience as a spiritual guide to assist others in tapping into a deeper connection with their intuition. She shares the value of and suggests ten paths for engaging in SoulWork Adventures, which are simple activities designed to be grounding and enjoyable and insightful. A cautionary note: undertaking these SoulWork Adventures has been know to bring serenity, whimsy and thoughtful action into the life of the practitioner.

One Last Thing...

If you enjoyed this book or found it useful I'd be very grateful if you'd post a short review on Amazon.com. Your support really does make a difference and I read all the reviews personally so I can get your feedback and make this book even better.

Thank you again for your support!

Loretta McCarthy